Anti-Procrastination

How to Stop Laziness,
Become More Productive,
and Get Things done

Jeffrey Turpen

Your Gift!

We want to show our appreciation that you support our work,
so we have put together a gift for you.
Just visit the link on the last page of this book to download it
now.
We know you will love this gift.
Thanks!

Table of Content

Introduction

In this book, we will discuss a problem that is often underestimated by many people, namely Procrastination, or "delay syndrome."

Do not be frightened, it's not a serious illness, a virus or something, but it's just a mental attitude that leads to waste a lot of time, postponing any project and ultimately leads to very few results, poor self-esteem and lose a lot of opportunities.

I'm sure that at least once in your life you have been a procrastinator, it's a normal thing, I was (and maybe I'm still) a procrastinator, I have a drawer full of great projects (a bestselling book, a revolutionary project, the plan to conquer Wthe world, train to the gym every day) that I never realized, but in the end I was able to take notice of the problem and decided to solve it.

Procrastination can be defeated but requires determination and willpower; it will be a war that you will have to fight alone, I do not want to lie, it will be challenging, and you will have a relapse, will require sacrifice and commitment, but eventually, you will get clear and visible results.

What results will you get?

- Your self-esteem will increase.
- Finally, you will realize every project
- You will learn to be more productive
- You will learn how to manage time better
- You'll have more time for others

- You will lose many bad habits

If you are interested in changing your life, read this book. Otherwise, I'm sorry for the trouble; you can continue to study the day before the exam, to be always tired, never to have time for anyone, to lose precious time in useless activities. Goodbye.

Ah, you're still here! Congratulations, you made the right choice.

Together we will change your life, stop the procrastination and find that it was straightforward if you know how to do it.

Chapter 1: What is Procrastination?

First, we must know our enemy.

Procrastination is a problem, not a disease. Procrastination is an attitude, a lifestyle and you cannot eliminate this issue with a magic pill or a medicine, so avoid paying attention to those who sell miraculous drugs against this problem, because in the best cases this is only a Placebo effect (A useless drug or remedy that our mind feels is effective) or a scam.

There is no magic pill to solve this problem, and as in many other problems, there is no simple solution. Be always diffident on those who offer simple solutions to complex problems.

To resolve procrastination, time, willpower, and sacrifice is needed. I know that I have already written it, but it is a concept that I will never tire of repeating and it is valid for other problems in our lives. People who are waiting for the magic solution, something falling from the sky and able to change their lives are destined to fail.

So if someone has offered you an Anti- Procrastination medicine call the police right away, it's a scammer.

Procrastination by extending the concept means bringing laziness to extreme levels.

Here are some practical examples:

You have to study for the exam but spend your time chatting, browsing the Internet and watching kittens video. You know you have to study, but your answer is always "I still have time." Then one morning you wake up, you will notice that the exam is very close and you will have to study all night long, you will arrive tired to the exam, and the examination will be a significant failure.

You will look for a culprit, and you will have to accept your procrastination or change this habit.

You have an excellent idea, a revolutionary App, able to compete with WhatsApp, Instagram, and Twitter.

The idea needs to be developed, you have to create a marketing plan, promote, hire developers, designers, beta testers, invest money, but you're sure of the success of your idea.

But you are tired tonight; you will begin to plan everything.

Tomorrow you'll have other things to do.

Then on the weekend, you want to go to the disco.

Then you'll forget the idea and some other person will realize your project.

The procrastination, this instinct to postpone everything has destroyed an exciting project. For what? Lost time, dissatisfaction, a fall in self-esteem.

Want to go to the gym to lose weight, be in physical shape and meet new people. You're ready, you bought the equipment, bought vitamins sponsored by Arnold Schwarzenegger, you've already paid the subscription. You just have to start.

But today you are tired after work; you will begin.

Then forget the bag at home.Then you decide to start Monday.

Then you will never go to the gym, and you will become fat. You will not know anyone, and you will be in a bad physical form.You've lost money, and you've been a stupid. Thank you procrastination.I could list other examples, but I'm sure you understood the problem.

Hence, procrastination is the attitude of postponing every time the activities that we find annoying, tedious, which do not interest us or that awaken our fears.

A person who procrastinates puts into practice a form of avoidance that allows him not to come into contact with his insecurities, fears, and limitations.

Doing so does not address some concerns and is not bound to have to deal with the emotions that derive from it.

There are at least two different styles of procrastination, one defined Relaxed and the other worried.

The relaxed procrastinator is the one who avoids activities considered dull and routine. It entices many activities with enthusiasm, but once the new effect is finished, it tends to get tired and to give up.

The worrying procrastinator is instead the one who tends to have little confidence in his abilities, has difficulty managing the stress, and is often tormented by a series of irrational fears and ideas that do not allow him to act.

The procrastination, therefore, has some cognitive features:

1. Perfectionism: the person does not feel able to face a task or problem if he fails to do it perfectly. You never feel quite ready or sufficiently confident in your abilities, knowledge or skills.

2. Fear of failure: Many refer infinitely the things they would want to do for fear of failure. This fear can sometimes be so strong to block any initiative by basing this behavior on the belief that you will get a bankruptcy or a big failure and for this, it does not even try.

3. Fear of success: who is afraid of success is a person who feels he/she do not deserve it and therefore lives in a state of guilt or may have the fear that others will then always expect satisfactory performance from he/she and thus live these expectations with strong anxiety and stress. A kind of performance anxiety, your audience always awaits a masterpiece, and you are afraid of failing.

4. Anger: This is often a response to the pressures and expectations of others who have lived as intolerable. If not recognized, it can become a serious problem that could invade different areas of life. Managing anger is a serious problem, coming out of procrastination (avoiding activities that might make us angry) and deserve a dedicated book.

In short, procrastination can lead to different consequences until, in extreme cases, compromise the overall functioning of those who put it to practice continuously.

These words make us understand that procrastination is a problem inside our head, which we have to solve with the help of a professional (in the most severe cases) and our willpower (again).

Before continuing, however, I want to clarify a concept: pauses are NECESSARY. We are not machines that can work regularly. Our brain and body require a break (the idea of the Clockwork Tomato is beneficial in this way, a break every 25 minutes of activity). But these breaks do not have to be an excuse to don't work or to waste time.

Watching an episode of a TV series or spending an hour on YouTube is not a bad habit if we've finished our daily work or if we can handle it, but it becomes a problem when the break becomes an activity that can occupy our entire day relegating the true work in a corner.

So it's okay to stop, have a break, but do not overdo it.

"The right one is in the middle," said the ancient Romans.

Chapter 2: The Role of Willpower

Once again, the principal architect of change is you. If you do not want to change any therapy can improve the situation.

Just like an alcoholic, if you do not want to change it is useless to try. So, unless we use force as in "A Clockwork Orange" will power is needed to overcome procrastination.

Some people are born with a great willpower within them, a unique talent, the ability to never give up and end any project.

They do not need to develop this talent because they already have it. But not everyone is born with the willpower of a, so the willpower needs workout (like a muscle) and needs to be developed with particular exercises.

Let's look at the most useful.

1. Develop a reasonable goal and a work plan which allows achieving the aim. So, no unrealistic goals, but start with straightforward and concrete things such as do ten push-ups every night and read a few pages of a book.

2. Create a list of powerful motivations that will lead to the set goal. You need to read this list every morning, and every time you are tempted to abandon the target, too, and especially when you do not want to do it. Motivations must be practical as "exam" "Otherwise you will become fat" "Want to impress your partner."

3. Recognize the dedication whenever you engage in behaviors designed to reach the established goal and avoid actions that, on the contrary, keep away from the pursuit of purpose. A prize is a good motivation.

4. Set up a daily list of things to accomplish, which will make you uncomfortable if you fail to complete it. An efficient method is to enter the indispensable comportment, such as buying food, cooking, disposing of garbage.

5. Do not bother yourself with sabotaging thinking, or let it slide into your mind while keeping your target. By putting in the list behaviors, you will not be able to sabotage yourself.

6. Identify obstacles and solve problems in advance, knowing that coming out of the set work plan is easy to engage in endless temptations. Avoid distractions and improvisation, at least until you have developed a strong willpower.

7. Prepare to face the feelings of discouragement, disappointment, and deprivation that arise when you are unable to meet your goal. You have to hate those feelings and not want to feel them again.

8. Decide how to reward yourself when you reach your goals and sub-goals. Choose a generous prize, which can be repeated every time, avoid cakes and expensive cars.

9. Focus on the experiences that are worth doing to facilitate the achievement of the goal. Typically, activities related to your goals.

10. Return to point number 1 when you go "off track."

These strategies are critical to keep up and amplify motivation and willpower when they will inevitably tend to diminish.

When the game is tough, motivation and willpower begin to play.

These methods are "active" methods that require your physical participation.

They can not be realized without your physical involvement and therefore are the first step to get out of the tunnel of procrastination and the habit of postponing everything to tomorrow.

You have to get used to being personally involved because the intervention has to be done inside your head, so you will have to face your character and fears, and win this match.

And if you do not start striking first it will be difficult to win. A match is won by attacking, not remaining in defense and waiting for who knows what.

So, first you perfect your willpower, and then go to the next chapter; otherwise, it is like to face a Tyrannosaurus Rex armed with a fork.

Chapter 3: How to Fight Procrastination

Now you are determined, you have a willpower able to move the mountains, Procrastination has counted days!

The Procrastination is within us, in our heads, so you'll be prepared to change your habits, get out of your comfort zone and take action.

Did you expect an easy and fast method?

I'm sorry, I have already written that there are no easy solutions to any problem, including that of procrastination.

If you have succeeded in developing willpower, then this should not be an issue for you, but I wanted to clarify this concept once again.

If you do not have a strong willpower I'm sorry, you will never be able to defeat this monster, regardless of your commitment.

Then go back to the previous chapter, take some time to reinforce your willpower and then come back here.

You can not fight a war against an army armed with a stick; you must have the humility to recognize it.

So get up from your couch, unplug all electronic devices and start kicking off the Procrastination!

Before I begin, I want to clarify something else.

These methods are active, require your commitment and your dedication, they are exercises in self-analysis and require SINCERITY.

Do not think that everything is fine and do not be afraid to write your problems and all your mental blocks. No one has the right to judge you for that, and no one should think he's better than you.

If you can not be honest with yourself in this self-analysis, then all work is completely useless because you will work on a partial evaluation and you will never focus on the real problem.

Be honest is very difficult, at some moments of our lives is harmful, especially in this extremely competitive society, but you must be frank with yourself, you don't have to live in an imaginary world where everything is perfect, and there are no problems.

Instead, problems exist, the elephant in the room is bright and visible. Ignoring problems has never produced good results.

So abandon fear and pride and recognize your limitations, will be the first step to eliminate them.

Find reasons.

First, you have to have strong motivations to stop procrastinating. Think about your project, exam, gym, what you want, everything you have not been able to accomplish because you've postponed each time because you've lost time in unnecessary activities.

The question you need to get in front of the mirror is this:

"If I was able to realize all my projects, now my life will be better?"

Take a sheet of paper and write the answer.

Imagine yourself with graduation, with a personal project, with a nice six-pack. Do not limit your fantasy; you have to imagine the best possible life.

Then ask yourself the second question, the most important one

"If from now on I had the discipline and the perseverance to start and continue the activities I consider necessary for achieving individual goals, how could my reality be different in 5 years?"

Write the answer on the sheet of paper. Surely the two responses are similar or the same.

That sheet must trigger something inside your head, a desire to act, a voice that says "I'm tired, I want to change."

Hang the sheet in a visible place and consult it every day, should be your primary motivation.

Write also all your fears on a new piece of paper and then burn it.

This system is highly scenic and motivational. Writing your fears is useful to visualize them in your mind and realize that most of your fears are just limits that lead you to procrastinate (fear of failure, fear of success, fear of anger or suffering).

Burning them means erasing them, abandoning them.

You can not undertake a process of abandoning procrastination if you are still afraid of something that does not exist and that is just inside your head.

If you believe this method is stupid, a famous character used it often, an athletic, strong, invincible person, an example of behavior for millions of fans around the world even nearly 50 years after his death.

A man named Bruce Lee.

Identify the area.

The most desperate cases of procrastination can postpone anything in every area of their lives (and in this instance, you do not need a book, but a professional medical aid), while the "classic" procrastinator procrastinates only a few "areas" of his/her life.

Think about it, you always procrastinate the gym, but you can always find 10 minutes to watch a video on YouTube, or you don't have any problem reading a comic, but it's impossible to study.

Lists all the areas where you procrastinate, usually those areas are two.

- Do you procrastinate housework?

- Do you procrastinate work-related or school-related activities?

- Do you delay activities related to your relationship with others, for example, postpone co-existence or avoid a serious relationship?

- Procrastinate any activities related to your health live check-ups and regular visits to the doctor (the most stupid thing in my opinion)?

Set yourself a goal.

To stop procrastinating you first need a goal, something that will push you to act and exit your comfort zone.

The objective must have some features:

- It must be easy to be done without too much effort (to start, then you can go to more complex goals).

- It must be something you want to do. You can not have the purpose of playing the guitar if you do not know anything about music. The only result you achieve is frustration and failure.

- It must be specific. A general goal is excellent, but a specific goal is more useful. "I want to do abs every day" is more effective than "I want to train every day."

Once the first goal is achieved (the most difficult obstacle) you can go to more complex goals since you will be able to defeat many bad habits and have a lot more self-esteem. Yes, you can also take guitar lessons or conquer the world.

Having a deadline for the goal is imperative. The deadline can be very stressful, but it is necessary to avoid an endless procrastination and to foster a sense of duty. The deadline must always be respected unless there are unforeseen events that can destroy a project (a failure of the PC, illness, personal problems).

Identify the problem.

Take the paper and, after thinking carefully, write down the causes that push you to procrastinate, all those activities that prevent you from achieving your goal.

Here, too, the maximum sincerity is required.

Usually, the leading causes are:

- stress

- afraid of failing

- overloaded with things to do

- laziness

- lack of motivation

- lack of discipline

- bad time management

- perfectionism

- avoid unpleasant activities.

Writing these mental blocks will help you look at their true essence, they are just limits in your head trying to block you.

Bruce Lee wrote his fears and limitations on the sheet of paper and then burned it, to symbolize the overcoming of his fears, in our case, it's enough to write them on the sheet even if burning the sheet is very scenic and motivational.

You will also realize that these mental blocks are simple to overcome with the right method, changing your habits and working system.

For example, if the factor that blocks you is "I have too many commitments" you can split the project into a set of smaller and easier to manage commitments to start the anti-procrastination path.

I repeat it again, sincerity is essential on this route, no one will judge you for your actions, and so you are free to write your fears.

Nobody is Rambo or Terminator, a man without any fear though everyone would want to communicate that image to other people and have no right to feel superior to you. A person who can communicate his fears is much more courageous than an individual who hides them and tries to pretend they do not exist.

So do not be scared and dug inside of yourself, the answers are there.

Neutralizes time losses.

Distractions are the strongest weapon of procrastination, all the activities that lead us to waste a lot of time and do nothing. In this technological era, distractions are more powerful than ever. One minute on Facebook, one minute on Twitter, one minute on Instagram, Reddit and YouTube and you've lost a lot of time.

I repeat (they are boring) distractions are not "EVIL, " but they become dangerous when they take too long and affect the quality of our lives and our work.

In that case, they are not just pastimes but a distraction to stop as soon as possible to be finally productive.

List all the activities that slow your work and your study into the paper sheet so that you have a list of your enemies.

Try to answer these questions.

What were you thinking about before postponing your business?

What did you focus on?

How do you justify your behavior?

What apologies did you use?

What happened in the environment?

What are the alternative activities you have decided to do?

These questions are fundamental to understand your enemy and to take the necessary countermeasures. Being distracted and thinking about something else during work is normal but it does not have to be a priority. First, you have to finish the job, and then you can think of a hobby or other activity.

Always try to avoid multitasking because it is just a way to make mistakes in several activities at the same time.

As for the electronic distractions, it is better to adopt a drastic attitude, so switch off your smartphone or disabled all the notifications for the duration of your project.

Use an App like Freedom to prevent access to certain sites (for example, to all social networks) for a given period, thus eliminating electronic distractions, a great ally of the modern procrastinator.

Details

Sometimes having a goal and a deadline are not enough to let us finally act and beat procrastination, so many "details" are needed to help us be motivated in our project.

Then, select your first project and begin to plan in detail everything you need to do to complete it.

Think "who, what, how, when, because" all the necessary information must be written on the sheet and must become a clear path in your mind that can help you in your struggle against procrastination.

The researchers found that the procrastinators that specify the actions needed to accomplish their goal have eight times more chance of starting a task compared with the procrastinators who do not use them. For example, instead of saying "I'll do some physical activity every day," you can say, "every night at 7 pm I'll be doing 15 minutes of jogging."

Show progress

Now you have all the data you need, you can no longer say that you do not know how to realize your project, so now you just have to act.

In this case, it is imperative to show the progress you are getting to stay motivated. Mark the deadline for your project on the calendar and write down your progress each day, making it easy to see how easy it is to avoid procrastination.

The habit of recording progress is beneficial, especially for athletes. Making daily photos of your physics is very useful to note muscle development and continue to go to the gym.

Chapter 4: Some Useful Tricks

Now you know how to stop procrastinating according to the tips in the previous section, but here are some other interesting tricks to keep concentration, to be motivated, able to transform the "postponement" into "doing."
The first is the motivation, already discussed above.
 You have to keep in mind your ultimate goal and always be optimistic (The exam will be a success,
 I will have a body like Schwarzenegger, I'll write a best seller) to have the motivation to go ahead and keep acting.
Never stop thinking about your goal, as time goes by, you will find that it will be an increasingly natural thought.
Attention: always thinking about the goal and doing the best to achieve it does not ensure its success, but it is always better to stay on the couch and never try to make something in your life.
Stop procrastinating does not guarantee the success, but it greatly increases chances of doing something.
The second trick is to reward your progress. Eat ice cream, buy a dress or a book, a little vacation, but give yourself a prize for every goal achieved. This award will help you stay motivated, and the brain will associate a positive reaction to your activities.

If you want, you can eliminate these small gifts at the time, but at the beginning of the journey they are beneficial and have a motivational function that can not be underestimated.

The third trick, modify your language, what you use to talk with yourself and motivate you.

The language that it uses internally plays a significant role in procrastination (and not just in that activity).

"I have to finish this task for 10."

"I should go to the gym to lose 5 pounds."

"I must read this book."

Remember that expressions like "I must," "I should," "I have to" communicate to your conflicting unconscious messages that evoke internal resistance. Unfortunately, these are often the words that procrastinators say to themselves to take action.

The secret is to talk to yourself in a motivating way, and you can do it by transforming the activity to be done in a choice or act of determination (I want, choose, I will go).

So "I need to enroll in the gym" can become "I want to join the gym because I want to feel more fit", "I have to finish this task for 10" could become "I choose to complete this task for 10 so you have much more free time to devote to my favorite activities "," I should go to the mechanic "in" I'll go to the mechanic. "

And finally, do not ever be discouraged, especially if you skip an activity for any reason. You do not have to be a machine, just lose your bad habits and make sure you do not fall into old vices.

Conclusion

Here's how to overcome procrastination. The work will be long and tiring, surely you will come back to procrastinate at some point, but the important thing is to make the first step and take the initiative. The pauses can be handled and the distractions blocked, what you have to change is just your mental approach to the problem.

Now you have all the tools you need; you can kick the procrastination out of your life!

Your Gift!

We want to show our appreciation that you support our work, so we have put together a gift for you.

bit.ly/2u7pdNL

Just visit the link above to download it now.

We know you will love this gift.

Thanks!